ABC

Candy Book

AO PRESS

Jessica Lee Anderson

Paperback ISBN: 978-1-964078-99-1

Photo credits—Front cover: A: Laimdota, B: peangdao, C: Maria Uspenskaya, arinahabich; Back Cover: ajafoto; Cover page: A: Laimdota, B: peangdao, C: Maria Uspenskaya, Billion Photos; Copyright page: Anastasia Turshina (sour strip candy), sanjels (heart candy); Dedication page: Billion Photos, p. 4: A: Denja1 (almond candies), LegART, fotogal, vikif; p. 5: B: David Tran (butterscotch candies), Victoria1988, dan_chippendale, Brand X Pictures; p. 6: C: Dusty Pixel (Candy Corn), Jupiter Images, maxlashcheuski, Realistic Design; p. 7: D: Elena Gurova (dulce de leche), Billion Photos, Cindy Shebley; p. 8: E: studioportosabbia (egg chocolates), One Pony, Paul D. Wade, MizC; p. 9: F: Sungsu Han (fruit hard candy), Billion Photos, Jupiter Images, Loulouvonglup; p. 10: G: ozgurkeser (gummy worms), Prostydio, FSTOPLIGHT; p. 11: H: Ruth Black (hard candy), tab1962, jallfree, mcmirjana; p. 12: I: egal (ice cream flavored marshmallows), jeehyun, Africa images, Heike Rau; p. 13: J: dndavis (jelly beans), Easybuy4u, WEKWEK, Sondra P; p.14: Handmade Pictures (key lime gummies), Peter Kai, Svetlana Monyakova, Handmade Pictures; p. 15: Ivonne Wierink (licorice allsorts), Russell Illig, Photology1971, kitiara75; p. 16: M: KADImages (mint candies), Layer-Lab, Billion Photos, Petasz; p. 17: N: Photografia Basica (nutty chocolates), Alessandra RC, Jorge_imstock, GarysFRP, p. 18: O: Billion Photos (orange lollipop), pixelshot, Svitlana Symonova Billion Photos; p. 19: P: Warren_Price (pecan pralines), bhofack2, tashka2000, arinahabich; p. 20: Q: jatrax (queen anne cherries covered in chocolate, Prostydio, manyakotic, BeyondTheRoad; p. 21: R: BWFolsom (raspberry candy), arcimages, Joe_Potato, BWFolsom, p. 22: S: praisaeng (sprinkles), Jupiterimages, AnVYChicago, riderfoot; p. 23: T: Yana Gavvoronskava (Turkish delight), Billion Photos, pakhnyushchyy; bdspnimage; p. 24: U: Laimdota (ultrasour candy strips), KADImages, lenazap, Tatyana Abramovich; p: 25: V: Brett_Hondow (violet candies), Billion Photos, mabaff, MGovantes, p. 26: W: Angela Colac (watermelon gummies), DreamBigPhotos, Billion Photos, liveslow; p. 27: X: ImagesByBarbara (X-treme sour candy), apugach, Hanna, Saaster; p. 28: Y: supitchamcsdam (yellow fruit sours), Aris Leoven, Anthony Rosenberg, M-Production; p. 29: Z: Africa images (zefir), anmbph, laperia_foto; ffolas; p. 30: Billion Photos, pixelshot, Billion Photos; p. 31: Michael Anderson

This Book Belongs to:

_____

A is for . . .

Apple Sours

Apricot Jellies

Almond Bark

A a

 **is for . . .**

Bubblegum

Bon Bons

Brittle

B b

5

C is for . . .

Cotton Candy

Caramel

Candy Canes

C c

 **is for . . .**

Dark Chocolate

Dark Chocolate Covered Raisins

Divinity

 **is for . . .**

Eyeball Candy

Egg Gummies

English Toffee

8

F is for . . .

Fruit Candy

Fudge

Flying Saucer Candy

F f

 **is for . . .**

Gummy Bears

Gummy Cola

Gum Drops

 **is for . . .**

**Heart-Shaped
Candy**

Honeycomb Candy

Hard Candy

H h

 **is for . . .**

Ice Cream Cone Gummies

Ice Cream Flavored Marshmallows

Ischoklad (also known as Ice Chocolate or Swedish Christmas Chocolate)

 **is for . . .**

Jelly Candies

Jelly Beans

Jordan Almonds

Jj

 **K** is for . . .

Kumquat Candy

Kiwifruit Candy

Key Lime Candy

L is for . . .

Lemon Drops

Licorice

Lollipops

L l

15

 **is for . . .**

Milk Chocolate

Maple Candy

Marzipan

 **is for . . .**

Nougat

Nonpareils

Nut Clusters

N n

 **is for . . .**

Orange Chocolate

Orange Slices

Orange Cream Hard Candy

 **is for . . .**

Peach Gummy Rings

Peanut Butter Cups

Pecan Turtle Candies

P p

19

 **is for . . .**

Queen Anne Cherries Covered in Chocolate

Quince Candy

Quinoa Chocolate Candy

20

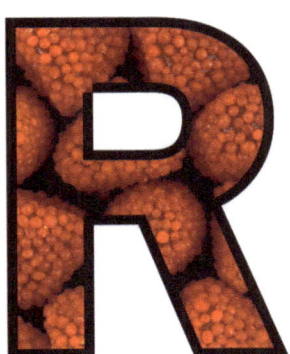 **is for . . .**

Rock Candy

Ribbon Candy

Red Licorice

R r

 **is for . . .**

Salt Water Taffy

Stick Candy

Sour Strawberries

22

T is for . . .

Toffee

Truffles

Turkish Delight

T t

 **is for . . .**

Ultra-Sour Candy

Ube Candy

Unicorn Lollipop

V is for . . .

Vanilla Caramel Fudge

Vanilla Marshmallows

Violet Candies

V v

 **is for . . .**

Walnut Fudge

White Chocolate

Watermelon Taffy

W w

X is for . . .

Xylitol Lollipops

Xylitol Mints

Xylitol Gum

X x

Y is for . . .

Yogurt Raisins

Yema

Yellow Banana Candies

 **is for . . .**

Zwetschge (Blue Plum) Jellies

Zefir

Zest Candy

Z z

5 Candy Facts:

 Candy dates back to ancient times with ingredients like honey, fruits, and nuts.

 Over a billion candy canes are sold every year!

 Chocolate bars are some of the most popular candies at Halloween.

 Cotton Candy is also known as Fairy Floss.

 Some candies can be made with sugar substitutes like xylitol (which can be toxic to dogs).

Jessica Lee Anderson is an award-winning author of over 50 books for young readers. Jessica lives near Austin, Texas with her daughter, Ava, and husband, Michael. Chocolate is one of Jessica's favorite types of candy. You can learn more about Jessica by visiting www.jessicaleeanderson.com.

Check out these other titles:

ABC
Pet Care Book

Jessica Lee Anderson

ABC
Fruit Book

Jessica Lee Anderson

ABC
Reptile Book

Jessica Lee Anderson